Seven Simple card Spreads

to celebrate
your creative wins

Also by Mariëlle S. Smith

52 Weeks of Writing Author Journal and Planner, Vol. I: Get out of your own way and become the writer you're meant to be

52 Weeks of Writing Author Journal and Planner, Vol. II: Get out of your own way and become the writer you're meant to be

52 Weeks of Writing Author Journal and Planner, Vol. III: Get out of your own way and become the writer you're meant to be

365 Days of Gratitude Journal: Commit to the life-changing power of gratitude by creating a sustainable practice

365 Days of Gratitude Journal, Vol. II: Commit to the life-changing power of gratitude by creating a sustainable practice

Fleshing Out the Narrative: A 31-Day Tarot and Journal Challenge for Writers

Get Out of Your Own Way: A 31-Day Tarot Challenge for Writers and Other Creatives

Set Yourself Up for Success: A 31-Day Tarot Challenge for Writers and Other Creatives

Seven Simple Spreads 1: Seven Simple Card Spreads to Unlock Your Creative Flow

Seven Simple Spreads 2: Seven Simple Card Spreads to Direct Your Creative Flow

Seven Simple Spreads Book 3: Seven Simple Card Spreads to Boost Your Creative Confidence

Speak Your Truth: A 31-Day Tarot Challenge for Writers and Other Creatives

Step into Your Power: A 31-Day Tarot Challenge to Unleash Your Creative Potential

Tarot for Creatives: 21 Tarot Spreads to (Re)Connect to Your Intuition and Ignite that Creative Spark

Co-written under the pen name Heather MacLee

Too Good to Be True?

Where There's a Will

There's a Way

Seven Simple Spreads Book 4

Seven Simple card Spreads

to celebrate
your creative wins

Mariëlle S. Smith

ISBN 978 94 93250 31 4

The Four of Wands

INTRODUCTION

Welcome to the journey that is *Seven Simple Spreads*! I'm so glad we'll be walking down our creative paths together.

Seven Simple Spreads is a ten-part series that follows the creative journey as told by the ten numbered cards of the suit of Wands, one of the four suits that make up the tarot's minor arcana. Each part, or step, of this journey zooms in on a different card, from the Ace of Wands to the Ten of Wands.

Using the chakra system as a map, each single step will take you past the seven main chakras. As such, there are seven different spreads for each of the ten steps: one spread for each chakra. In total, the *Seven Simple Spreads* series consists of seventy spreads.

Because all steps of the creative journey come with their own struggles, the seven spreads included in each will help you:

- discover what's hindering you on each chakra level on that part of the journey; and
- how you can overcome those chakra-specific obstacles.

Before we dive into the set of spreads that come with this step of the journey, let me explain how the *Seven Simple Spreads* series came to be.

Creativity and cartomancy

Generally speaking, cards—whether from a tarot, oracle, or angel deck—can be applied to any and all aspects of our lives. I say 'generally speaking', because there are decks that are designed with a particular purpose or theme in mind. That doesn't necessarily mean they can no longer be used in other areas, but it does make it less straightforward to do so.

Being a creative who works with other creatives, it's no wonder I turn to my cards to explore and answer questions around creative pursuits, struggles, and purposes. I don't know whether there's anything special about the relationship between creativity and cartomancy, but I do know they are a great match in practice. Unsurprisingly perhaps, since the reading of cards is in itself, like the making of art, a creative and intuitive endeavour.

Creativity and chakra philosophy

Over the years, I've been blessed with immensely talented and knowledgeable yoga teachers and more than one has taught me all they know about chakras. It was Denise de With, one of my earliest mentors, who first introduced me to chakra philosophy. I am forever grateful to her for opening that door and for introducing me to Anodea Judith's work on the chakras.

It was Judith's *Creating on Purpose: The Spiritual Technology of Manifesting Through the Chakras*, which she wrote with Lion Goodman, that helped me to truly envision how the seven main chakras influence each and every step of the creative journey. In particular, it was their explanation of the two different currents that run through our chakras that enabled me to organise the ten sets of spreads in the series in the way I have.

As they succinctly explain, we tend to focus on the upward current of the seven main chakras. From the root chakra, we move up, through the navel, the solar plexus, the heart, the throat, and the third eye, until we reach the crown chakra at the top of the head. This is what Judith and Goodman call the current of liberation (Judith and Goodman 2012, 17). It's the path towards transcendence.

There are alternatives to this particular interpretation and I'm familiar with a few. For example, when I apply Reiki to heal myself or others, I move from the crown chakra to the root, because that's the order used within my Reiki tradition. However, and albeit it in different ways, both Elen Sentier, author of *Shaman Pathways—the Celtic Chakras* (2013), and Elizabeth Clare Prophet, author of *Violet Flame: Alchemy for Personal Change* (2016), argue that the connection between the main chakras should be visualised as a spiral instead of a linear path.

As such, it didn't necessarily turn my world upside down that Judith and Goodman bring up another path from the ascending current of liberation we're so familiar with: the descending *current of manifestation*. Where the current of liberation will free us from the material plane through transcendence, the descending current of manifestation is needed to turn our ideas into reality. However, what did turn my world upside down was their suggestion that we need both currents.

When doing research for *Seven Simple Spreads*, I realised that Judith already touches upon this idea briefly in her *Eastern Body, Western Mind: Psychology and the Chakra System as a Path to Self*. There, she explains how Eastern philosophies perceive transcendence, the 'expansion of consciousness', as the ultimate goal (Judith 2004, 408). However, she stresses that '[e]ventually we have to come back down as expansion of the consciousness is of greatest value when applied' (ibid.). After all, '[c]reation is the expression of the divine, and it is often more profound, refined, and detailed than the source itself, which is enormously vast and abstract' (408–9).

In other words, we do have to move upwards if we truly want to know our higher purpose, but we also need to come back down again to be able to fulfil said purpose. We need to move upwards to understand the why of our creative journey, and move back down to manifest the what.

As I mentioned earlier, each step on our creative journey has its own struggles. Some steps along the way need us to free ourselves from anything that's trying to keep us small so we can align ourselves with our higher purpose and reach our true potential. Other steps require us to work through what's preventing us from moving our aligned self forward so we can, in Judith's words, express the divine in a concrete way.

Creativity and the suit of Wands

All cards in whichever deck can speak to the creative journey depending on the questions you ask of that deck. In the tarot, however, it is the suit of Wands—or its equivalent in a tarot deck that uses alternative names for the four suits—that is explicitly concerned with creativity, passion, inspiration, and so on. Its element is fire, which can help us forge anything, if used constructively.

When I look at the numbered cards in the suit of Wands, I see a perfect blueprint for the creative journey. Starting with the Ace, which reminds us to invite inspiration into our lives, the suit of Wands demonstrates the steps needed to fulfil our purpose. From leaving our comfort zones to celebrating our first win, to spreading our wings fully and learning whom to invite feedback from, to learning to trust the process when there are no guarantees we will actually succeed—it's all there.

What is more, the journey from the Ace to the Ten of Wands depicts that constant dance between the upward and downward currents running through our seven main chakras. For example, the first set of spreads in the *Seven Simple Spreads* series follows the current of liberation: the Ace of Wands speaks to feeling inspired, being truly creative, and any blocks we might be experiencing on that level. To truly open up that channel, we have to move from our root to our crown chakra so we can free ourselves from all that is keeping us from envisioning and understanding our higher potential.

But, once we have opened up that channel and our inspiration knows no more bounds, we need to decide what we want to do with all that energy and where best to direct it. That creative spark needs to be turned into something real and tangible, and the Two of Wands invites us to map it all out. And so, the journey progresses, all the way to the Ten of Wands.

Once I made that connection, I couldn't unsee how we move from liberation to manifestation and back as we advance from one card to the next in this particular suit. However, the way you interpret these currents, the suit of Wands, and their connection may differ greatly from the way I understand them. That is why you should feel free to use the spreads in this series in whichever way and and order feels right to you.

No matter how you decide to work with the spreads this series offers, just know they are intended to set you free while helping you manifest your wildest creative desires. So, pick your favourite deck, whether tarot, oracle, or angel, and embrace this journey.

One step at a time.

THE FOUR OF WANDS

Seven simple card spreads to celebrate your creative wins

The fourth part of this ten-part series concentrates on the Four of Wands.

Those risks you've been taking over the past three cards? By the time you've made it to the Four of Wands, they will have started to pay off. Which makes it the perfect moment to enjoy and celebrate just how far you've come.

The Four of Wands is such a positive card, yet so many creatives struggle with its message. After all, we're not even halfway through the journey, so what is there to celebrate? Indeed, slowing down to take stock and savour the moment might seem counterproductive when we have such a long way to go still.

To me, this card serves as a reminder that it's about the journey and not the destination. The seven spreads in this set help us check in with each of the main chakras to find out what's keeping us from celebrating every creative step on the path, no matter how tiny, and how we can allow those wins to sustain us as we move forward.

Seven Simple Card Spreads to Celebrate Your Creative Wins follows the current of manifestation. Starting with the crown and our limiting beliefs about what does and doesn't count as a creative win, the spreads in this set move down to the root chakra to teach us how to enjoy and celebrate even the smallest of creative victories.

'I BELIEVE IN HONOURING MY EVERY WIN'

Sahasrara – Crown chakra

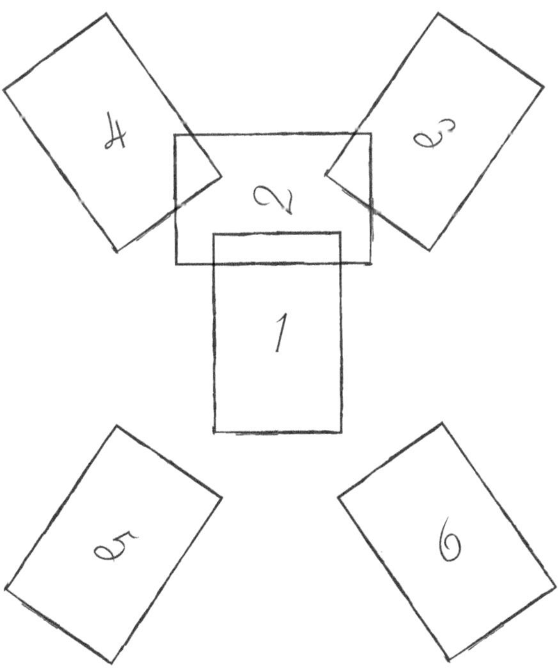

1. What limiting beliefs do I have about what is and isn't a creative win?
2. What limiting beliefs do I have about celebrating my creative wins?
3. Where do these beliefs come from?
4. How did I become attached to these beliefs?
5. How can I begin to let these beliefs go?
6. What do I want to believe about my creative wins and their celebration from this day on?

'I SEE THE NEED FOR CELEBRATION'

Ajna – Third eye chakra

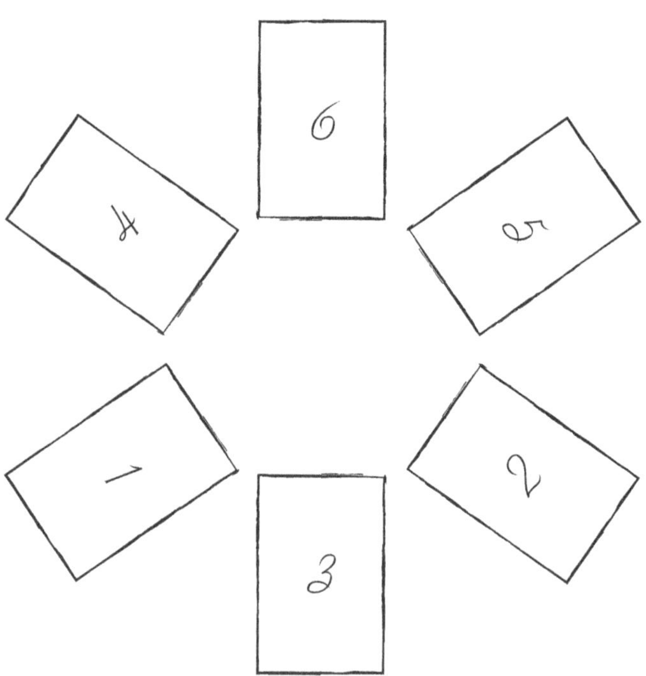

1. What illusions do I have about what is and isn't a creative win?
2. What illusions do I have about celebrating my creative wins?
3. Where do these illusions come from?
4. Why did I begin to believe in these illusions?
5. How can I begin to clear my vision from these illusions?
6. How do I want to envision my creative wins and their celebration from this day on?

'I SPEAK UP ABOUT MY CREATIVE WINS'

Vishuddha – Throat chakra

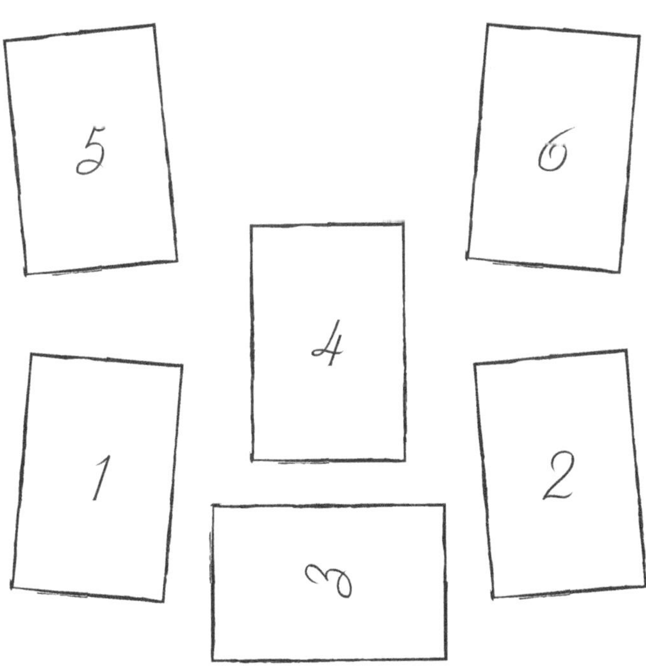

1. What lies do I tell myself about being open about my creative wins?
2. What lies do I tell myself about celebrating these creative wins openly?
3. Where do these lies come from?
4. Why did I start uttering these lies myself?
5. How do I truly feel about openly communicating and celebrating my creative wins?
6. How do I start speaking these truths to myself and the world?

'I SHARE MY CREATIVE WINS WITH THOSE I LOVE'

Anahata – Heart chakra

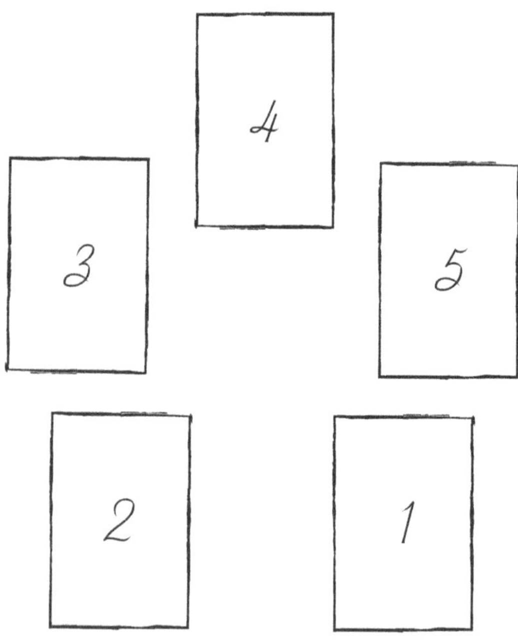

1. What hurts do I have around sharing my creative wins with my community?
2. What hurts do I have around celebrating these creative wins with my community?
3. Where do these hurts come from?
4. How do these hurts affect how I connect with others over my creativity?
5. How can I share and celebrate my creative wins with those I love from a place of love and acceptance?

'I AM CONFIDENT ABOUT MY CREATIVE WINS'

Manipura – Solar plexus chakra

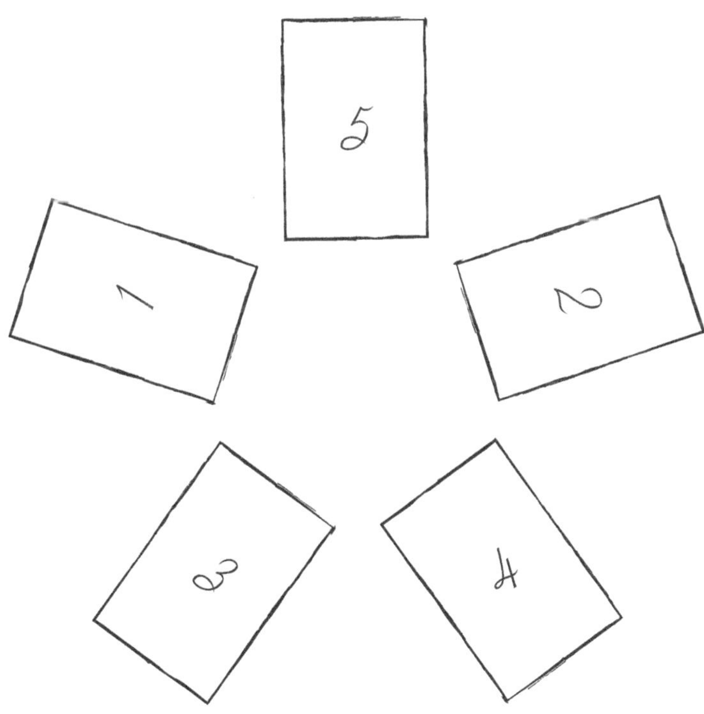

1. What shame do I feel around my creative wins?
2. What shame do I feel around celebrating these creative wins?
3. Where does this shame come from?
4. How can I begin to heal these feelings of shame?
5. How can I take back my power so I can be confident about my creative wins and how I choose to celebrate them?

'I FIND JOY IN CELEBRATING MY CREATIVE WINS'

Svadisthana – Sacral chakra

1. What guilt do I feel around my creative wins?
2. What guilt do I feel around celebrating these creative wins?
3. Where does this guilt come from?
4. How does this guilt block the flow of joy and pleasure into my creative life?
5. How can I begin to move away from these feelings of guilt?
6. How can I bring joy and pleasure to my creative wins and how I wish to celebrate them?

'I ACKNOWLEDGE AND CELEBRATE ALL OF MY CREATIVE WINS'

Muladhara – Root chakra

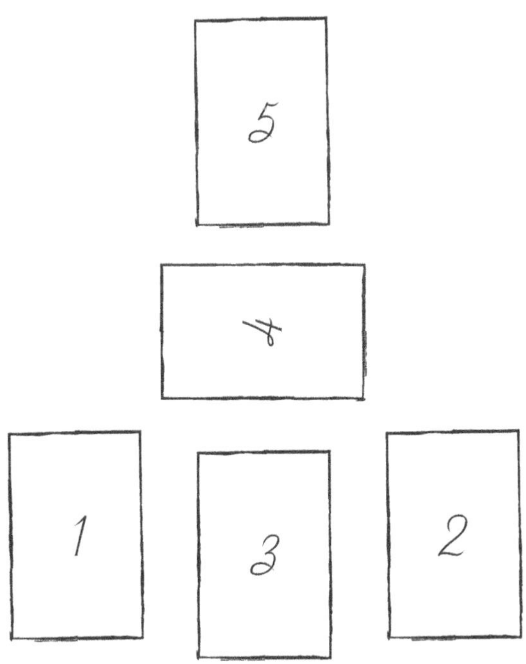

1. What fears do I have around my creative wins?
2. What fears do I have around celebrating those creative wins?
3. Where do these fears come from?
4. How do these fears keep me from enjoying my creative wins, no matter how small?
5. How can I transform these fears into the trust I need to fully acknowledge and celebrate all wins on my creative journey?

READY TO TAKE STOCK?

Jot down all your draws here and see what else...

	Spread 1	Spread 2	Spread 3
Q 1			
Q 2			
Q 3			
Q 4			
Q 5			
Q 6			
Q 7	X	X	X

LET'S CREATE AN OVERVIEW!

...there is to learn. Do you notice anything in particular?

Spread 4	Spread 5	Spread 6	Spread 7
X	X		X
X	X	X	X

BIBLIOGRAPHY

Judith, Anodea. *Eastern Body, Western Mind: Psychology and the Chakra System as a Path to the Self.* Berkeley: Celestial Arts, 2004.

Judith, Anodea, and Lion Goodman. *Creating on Purpose: The Spiritual Technology of Manifesting through the Chakras.* Boulder: Sounds True, 2012.

Prophet, Elizabeth Clare. *Violet Flame: Alchemy for Personal Change.* Gardiner: Summit University Press, 2016.

Sentier, Elen. *Shaman Pathways – the Celtic Chakras.* Ropley: John Hunt Publishing, 2013.

Please consider leaving a review

Authors are nowhere without honest reviews, and I'd truly appreciate it if you left one on Goodreads, my Facebook page facebook.com/mswordsmith, or the retailer where you bought this book.

The Creative Cardslingers

Isn't it better to sling cards together?

Join my private Facebook group The Creative Cardslingers (password **BUMBLEBEE JASPER**) to meet fellow creative cardreaders, be the first to test my latest card spreads, and hear all about the creative projects I'm involved in.

WANT MORE?

Head over to mswordsmith.nl/starterkit and get my free Get Out of Your Own Way Starter Kit now.

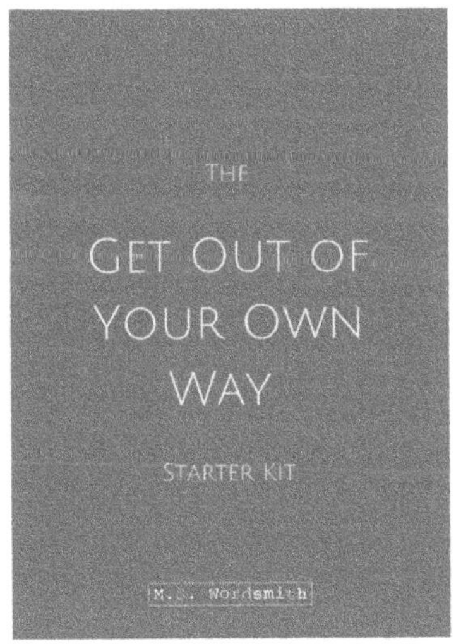

The Get Out of Your Own Way Starter Kit includes four different tools:

- An exercise on limiting beliefs,
- a monthly tracking and reflecting worksheet,
- a meditation on letting go of limiting beliefs,
- a tarot spread on creative roadblocks (from *Tarot for Creatives*),

and is yours when signing up to my newsletter.

ABOUT THE AUTHOR

That would be me!

I'm a coach for writers and other creatives, an editor, a writer, and a custom retreat organiser. Born in the Netherlands and raised by my Dutch mum and Scottish dad, I moved to the island of Cyprus in February 2019 to focus on my coaching, editing, and writing practice full-time.

It was here that I started to take my love for cardslinging seriously, and the *Seven Simple Spread* series is one of its many manifestations.

When not stuck behind my computer or bend over a card spread, I can be found exploring the island or on the beach, surrounded by the stray cats I feed.

Want to reach out? I'd love to hear from you!
You can find me here:

mswordsmith.nl
marielle@mswordsmith.nl
instagram.com/mariellessmith
facebook.com/mswordsmith

I WOULD LIKE TO THANK

Andri, for always wanting to celebrate even my smallest victories.

The Creative Cardslingers, for their endless support, ever-constructive feedback, and undying enthusiasm for everything I create.

www.ingramcontent.com/pod-product-compliance
Ingram Content Group UK Ltd.
Pitfield, Milton Keynes, MK11 3LW, UK
UKHW021651190726
13853UKWH00001B/191